Our Mom Has Cancer

Published by the
American Cancer Society
Health Content Products
1599 Clifton Road
Atlanta, GA 30329

5   4   3   2   1   00   01   02   03   04   05

ISBN 0-944235-31-X

Designed by Shock Design, Inc., Atlanta, Georgia

For more information, contact your American Cancer Society

at 1-800-ACS-2345 or www.cancer.org

Our Mom Has Cancer

Written and illustrated by
Abigail and Adrienne Ackermann

AMERICAN
CANCER
SOCIETY®

Hope. Progress. Answers.™

This book is dedicated to our mom, Dawn Ackermann

"Abby, Abby, look, there's our car! And Abby, there's Mom and Dad," Adrienne squealed with excitement.

We both got off the bus. We had just gotten home from a great week at summer camp! We chattered all the way home with our news. When we got home, Mom said to get ready for the luau at the pool. Our brother and sister had already gone on ahead.

1

"We want to talk to you about something," Mom said. From the look on Mom's face, it appeared that we were going to get bad news. Daddo then told us that they had had a hard week at home.

"Mom went to the doctor on Tuesday and found out she has breast cancer," Daddo explained.

Both of our mouths dropped open. Adrienne started to cry. All Abby could do was say "No" under her breath, but then she was crying too.

"Are you going to die?" Adrienne asked.

"Well, we're not planning on that, but I'll probably be sick for awhile," Mom said.

"How long?" asked Abby.

"Probably until Easter."

We cried for awhile and hugged Mom and Daddo. Then we went to the luau. We were glad to do something fun!

The time came for Mom's operation. Only Daddo went with her to the hospital.

We got to do something fun! We went to our cousin's house for a couple of days. We played games, watched movies, told stories, and had fun!

When we came home we rushed to greet Mom.

"Hold on," Mom said. "Hug me gently." She smiled.

For awhile Mom wore a sling on her arm. In the evenings we all did exercises with Mom, like stretching. Mom thought they were hard; we thought they were easy.

Usually in the summertime, lots of friends came to our house. Our mom would sometimes babysit them.

But this summer was different. Since our mom was feeling sick and she slept a lot, we visited lots and lots of friends instead. We had mixed feelings about that, but overall we had a LOT of fun!

At the end of the summer Mom started chemotherapy. It was bad.

The minute she came home after a day at the hospital with Daddo she went straight to bed. She couldn't eat with our family because the smell of the food would make her throw up. Adrienne would cry.

Mom would stay in bed for several days, laying very still. Instead of her coming to our room to say good night to us, we came to her bed to say good night to her. If she wasn't feeling too bad, she would still read to us.

11

After a few days Mom would start to feel better again and life seemed normal…except we were expecting her to lose her hair. Chemo does that.

One day we were sitting at the bus stop before school. Mom reached up to touch her hair and it came right out. If you put a piece of tape on it, the hair came right off! Pretty soon there were bald spots.

It was terrible! Really terrible!

13

Our aunt had a great idea. She threw a hat party for our mom! It was right after her hair was really falling out. Lots of friends came and everyone brought a hat!

We wrote a song and sang it. This is how it went…

There is dark hair and there's light
And there's hair that's out of sight
There is short hair and then there's long
But when all that hair falls out
Don't cry or weep or pout
'Cause a hat will cover up your scalp.

She had beautiful hair, beautiful hair
Hair that used to be there
But now her head is bare
But she had beautiful hair
And in the future she'll have beautiful hair!

Our mom was really pleased. She received thirteen hats!

Mom's hair was falling out so much she decided to shave it off and she said we could help. We went to our hairdresser Jessie's house. Jessie did most of it, but we did some, too.

Once Mom's head was totally shaved Abby exclaimed, "Mommy, you're all face!" We were happy to see that Mom didn't have a cone head, she had a perfectly round head. We took video pictures of the whole event.

17

One of the good things about Mom having cancer is all the wonderful dinners that our friends have been making for us.

Some of the foods we've had are lasagna, taco salad, soup, ribs, pork chops, and chicken. We asked people NOT to bring us any green beans. And they don't.

We really like the food because our mom never did particularly like to cook in the first place!

NO BEANS!

Halfway through Mom's treatments, the type of chemotherapy changed. We liked this kind better.

Instead of feeling sick in the beginning and good in the end, she felt good in the beginning and not so great in the end.

Instead of her stomach hurting, her bones hurt…especially her feet and legs. So, we got a wheelchair for those hard days. Although we wanted to push Mom more often, we made her nervous, so Daddo or our big brother did most of the pushing.

Now the chemotherapy treatments are over! Mom's hair is just starting to grow back. It feels like baby chick fuzz. Every time we hug her, we rub her head!

Before Mom's hair fell out it was blonde. Right now we don't know what color it will come in.

We are hoping it will come in red and curly. Our older brother and sister are hoping it will be blonde again.

But Mom and Daddo, especially Mom, wouldn't mind if she had GREEN hair, just as long as she has hair!

23

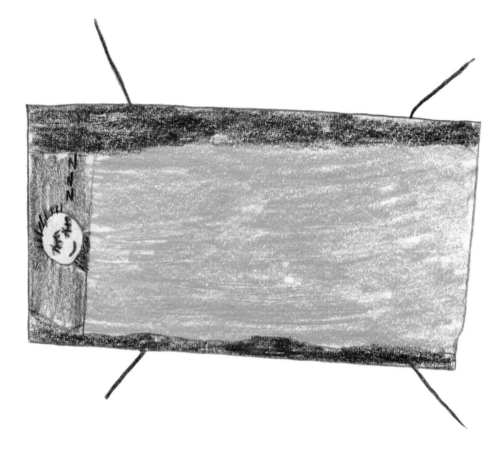

Pretty soon Mom will start radiation treatments. That means she'll be going to a hospital five days a week for six weeks. But she'll just be in there for about an hour a day.

She's not supposed to get sick, just tired. She'll go while we're in school. And her hair will keep growing!

In the beginning we both thought this experience would be terrible! But really, there have been some very good things about it.

We both enjoy wearing Mom's hats and eating those wonderful dinners.

Mom isn't as busy as she used to be.

Lots and lots of people have been praying for us and sending Mom lots of encouraging cards. We have a basket full of them!

Most of all, our family has gotten closer and closer through this experience.

About the Authors

Abigail Ackermann, age 11, is a 5th grader and Adrienne Ackermann, age 9, is a 4th grader at Thomas Pullen Magnet School for the Performing Arts in Landover, Maryland. They live with their 16-year-old brother, 14-year-old sister, parents, one dog, and one rabbit in Upper Marlboro, Maryland. They wanted to write this book to share their experience with other children.

For more information about cancer, contact your
American Cancer Society
at 1-800-ACS-2345 or www.cancer.org

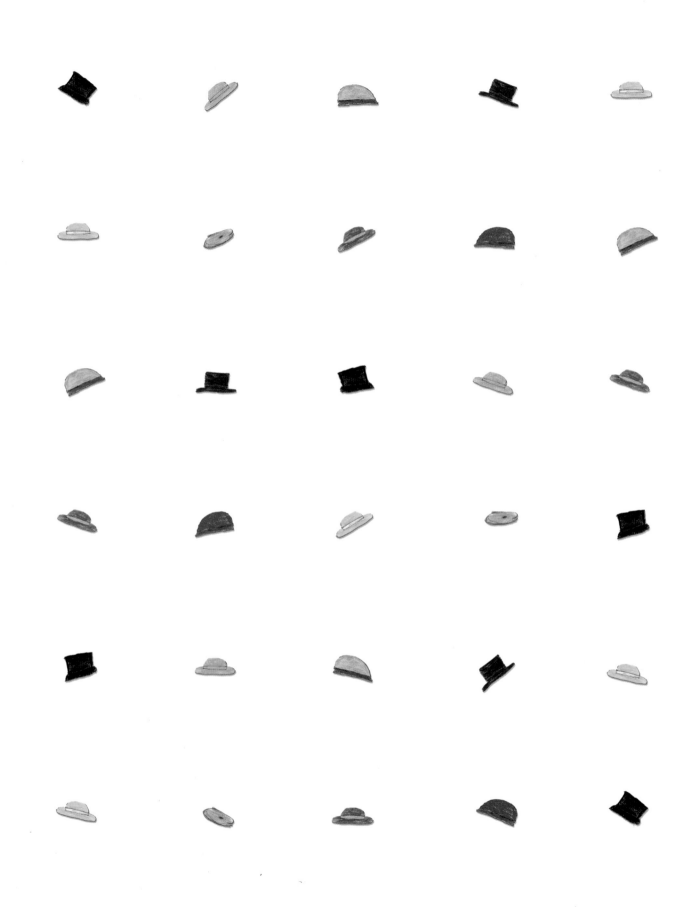